MW01077482

The Path to Enlightenment
 is not a Highway

The Path to Enlightenment is not a Highway

BABA HARI DASS

Edited by Ma Renu

SRI
RAMA

© 1996 by Sri Rama Publishing

Art Direction and Design: Dharani Dass
Design and Production: Kranti Mailliard
Photography: Anand Dass, Dharani Dass,
            Sumitra Peterson

Sri Rama Publishing
PO Box 2550 • Santa Cruz • CA 95063
*All rights reserved, including the right of
reproduction in whole or in part in any form.*
First printing, 1996
10   9   8   7   6   5   4   3   2   1
ISBN: #0-918100-18-6
Library of Congress Catalog Card No. 96-67104

SRI RAMA PUBLISHING is a non-profit organization
founded to produce the writings of Baba Hari Dass.
Profits from the sale of books and recordings are
used to support our orphanage in northern India.

Baba Hari Dass has kept a vow of silence since 1952 and has the gift of teaching by writing in concise and simple phrases. Starting in the Fall of 1994, in a small notebook entitled My Convictions, Babaji recorded these inspired insights as they came to him. For most of us the spiritual path is not a highway, often it is a steep and rocky road. We hope that reading Babaji's convictions, and reflecting on their universal truths will shed light on your path.

Ma Renu
December 1995

1	Bondage	191	Surrender
21	Desire	203	Yoga
31	Family & Community	211	Meditation
41	Art	225	Renunciation & Dispassion
47	Ego		
75	Mind	231	Self
93	Karma & Samskara	255	Silence
99	Death	261	Peace
107	Self-Development	269	Truth
131	Karma Yoga	285	Liberation
141	Love & Compassion		
155	Guru		
165	Devotion		

lly to all. Esto

t for everyone

houghts and ac

Bondage

y things you

ttached to the

eace within

This peace is

eep a calm or

The embodied soul

has two purposes to fulfill:

Experience the world, and

get liberation from all experiences.

If the self were not in bondage,

then the two purposes

would not be fulfilled.

Ignorance veils the mind

and gives rise to

egoism, attachment, and desires.

These fetters bind the soul

in the prison of the body.

A prisoner never stops thinking
about getting out of the prison.
Life in the world
is like sitting in a prison.
One who doesn't realize that
doesn't think of getting liberation.

The maladjusted ego within us
creates its own world
and binds itself with shackles
of attachment and passion.

It is not the gross body

that is in bondage,

but the owner of the body, the ego.

The ego creates its own bondage

by its nature of ownership.

When the idea of individuality

dawns in the mind,

the mind loses its identity with the real Self

and creates its own bondage.

To escape bondage,

the mind then seeks for the real Self,

which is always present and was never lost.

It is called bondage

when spirit and

the mind-body complex

are in a tight alliance as one.

Worldly allurements are hard to ignore;

the mind and senses are pulled

by the force of *samskaras* (conditioning).

Even those who disdain the world

get tricked.

Prosperity without, but no peace within

is simply living in hell.

In that hell

all objects of the senses

haunt the mind.

Hell and heaven are not 'out there.'

Living in restlessness and misery is hell;

living in undisturbed peace is heaven.

The mind-body complex

is a temple of God.

If this temple is not cared for properly,

it becomes a den of demons.

Present actions

will become past memories.

If one is possessed

by the sickness of lust now,

then what kind of future

and what kind of memories

can one hope for?

Your spiritual achievement
cannot be stolen by anyone,
but you yourself may lose it
by jumping in the mire of lust.

Anything can be a trap.

A hermit goes to a cave

to get out of all worldly attachments

and then gets attached to the cave.

If we miss the point,

then everything becomes a trap.

If you are expecting rewards

for your virtuous actions,

if your ears are eagerly waiting

to hear your praise,

if your words are expressing pride,

then be aware that you are falling

from the spiritual path.

Lofty dreams without enthusiasm,

a mind full of ideas with no practicality,

and dwelling in one's own philosophy,

which has no substance,

will take one nowhere.

Making separate groups
is human nature.
No matter how much we talk
about universal unity,
we end up making another group.

The ignorant and the wise,

both want to attain peace and happiness.

An ignorant person tries

to attain peace and happiness

through worldly objects

and creates more bondage.

The wise person attains peace

and happiness through knowledge

and achieves liberation.

Desire

lly to all. Esto
t for everyone
houghts and ac
for Desire gr
y things you
ttached to the
eace within
This peace is
eep a calm or

We enjoy worldly pleasures
but we are devoured by them,
because they cause greed
and discontentment.
If we don't identify ourselves
as the enjoyer,
then there is contentment.

Greed is a sickness of the mind.

The more one hoards,

the more greed increases.

Giving with no expectation

eliminates greed.

Desire to have more
causes stealing,
either by taking secretly
or by cheating.
By giving away things
to the needy,
the mind develops
desirelessness.

Fear accompanies ignorance

from birth to death.

Anything that is a source of enjoyment

becomes the source of fear,

because of the fear of losing it.

Desires never get old;

anything that is desired

always appears as new.

The desirer gets old,

but expectations never stop.

Desire is a cause of creativity.

When the waves of desire cease,

creativity also stops.

It's a state of silence

with no waves.

Desire is the cause of misery.

To become desireless,

the first step is to disassociate from objects.

The second step is to disassociate

from thoughts of objects.

The third step is to get rid of

the memory of past experience.

Renunciation
of egocentric desires
brings freedom
from all self-limitations.

Family and
Community

Human beings are tribal people by nature. They know for their survival they have to be supported by each other. So, like-minded people get together and make their own tribe. The tribe creates rules and a community is formed.

In the community, the main rules are to establish a sense of family, partnership, support, and selfless service. The spirit of the community is rooted in selfless service. A sense of family is established by working, playing, and eating together.

Each member of the community shares partnership in communal wealth and property.

Each member of the community is supported
by the community physically, psychologically,
and emotionally. Everyone works for the good
of the community, and the community works
for the good of everyone.

In this way, everyone shares an active,
industrious, and virtuous life and lives a well-
disciplined life, which brings every member
of the community together with a spirit of love
and cooperation.

Disciplined life, love, unity, and cooperation bring
success and remove all morbid feelings within an
individual, as well as in the community.

Marriage is sharing life
with your partner with love,
equality, and sacrifice.
Ideally the couple should love
each other unconditionally,
have equal rights, and sacrifice
their personal desires
for the good of each other.
It's a life-long commitment.

Household is a chariot.

The parents are its two wheels.

If the wheels don't move equally,

the chariot cannot run straight.

Children learn
by copying their parents.
If you want your child to be good,
then be good first.

Marriage is a karmic tie.

When two people

with complementary *samskaras* meet,

they are pulled closer

by the force of their *samskaras*.

Their love and attachment

bind them in a marriage.

Love and passion together

are the support of married life.

It binds two people

by creating attachment.

Otherwise the sense of unity

will not develop.

Rocky trails train us

to walk steadily, cautiously,

and carefully.

Hardship and difficulties

on the trail of life

bring out the best in us

and make us strong

and conscious.

A spirit of compromise is the key
to working in a community.

lly to all. Esto

t for everyone

houghts and a

for   e gr

y things   you

ttached to the

eace within

This peace is

eep a calm or

Poetry is a cry of the heart

or a song of love

written by the ink of tears,

in joy and sorrow.

It is a language of the heart.

Poetry is an offering

of inner feelings.

It is received by those

who listen to

the song of the heart.

Life is like acting.
Acting creates a reality
from the unreal;
you become that
which you are not.
This illusion is as real
as a mirage in a desert.

Dance

is a state of ecstasy

in which the body,

hands, and feet move

in a rhythmic gesture of emotions.

lly to all. Esto

t for everyone

houghts and ac

for   e gr

Ego

'y things you

ttached to the

eace within

This peace is

eep a calm m

The ego is the door of life
through which all desires
come in the mind and thrive
and make our world.

Just like pure water
poured in a dirty cup
becomes dirty,
similarly the pure ego
rooted in the impure mind
becomes impure ego.

The ego of impure mind
expresses its power and presence
in all negative thoughts,
events, actions, and emotions
more distinctly and forcefully
than the ego of positive mind.

The ego

of impure mind

acts in the world

by strife

and not by unity and harmony.

The ego functions

using the mind, intellect, and sense organs

as its instruments.

Desire, attachment, and sense objects

make its field of activity.

If the instruments and the field

are separated,

the ego becomes dormant.

The play of senses with sense objects
brings experience.
The experiences that are pleasing
to the mind create attachment,
those that are disliked create aversion.

The ego makes experiences
appear real.

The ego thrives

in evil thoughts, words, and deeds.

By cultivating truthfulness

in thoughts, words, and deeds,

the ego becomes dormant.

55

Egoism, attachment, and desires
are three heads of the same demon
who blocks the path of redemption.

Mind is the mother
of both virtue and vice.
Ego is the father,
who favors vice
to express ego's power.

One who truthfully listens to criticism
corrects his or her own mistakes.
One who doesn't listen truthfully
gets defensive.

The mind is a vessel of knowledge.

The ego through its sense of ownership

instigates action.

The ego colors the knowledge in the mind

by its nature of selfhood,

and that colored knowledge

turns to ignorance.

Selfish impulses weaken the will.
Then the ego becomes the ruler
and controller of life and
obstructs the path of liberation.

A mirror reflects a beam of sunlight.

If the mirror is rotated,

the beam of light also rotates.

The ego similarly reflects

the light of consciousness.

If the ego is restless, the

reflection of consciousness

in the mind will be distorted.

EGO

Ordinary people always assert their ego.

A wise person feels

it is all God's manifestation.

Ego is the cause of desires.

Attachment makes desires real.

Remove attachment

and the desires will become tasteless.

Ego is the notion of 'I am,'
but all identifications are different faces
of the same ego.

The ego has no form

and no particular center of existence.

It pervades the mind, intellect, senses,

and the body as 'I am.'

The ego has no form of its own,

yet the ego takes the form of anything

that is identified by the mind.

The actor and the action both exist

as long as the ego exists.

When the ego exists not,

then there is neither the actor nor the action.

Divine grace
doesn't dawn for a seeker
so long as the seeker
claims to be a performer.

The ego is a lifelong companion.

In childhood,

when the mind can't discriminate,

it appears as 'innocence.'

In adulthood,

when discrimination develops,

it appears as 'power.'

In old age,

when the mind gets weaker,

it appears as 'discontentment.'

At the time of death,

when mind and senses

start losing their powers,

it appears as 'helplessness.'

The subtle body and the soul

leave the gross body after death

and carry all the memories of the past

to the new birth.

But the ego relates to the new body

only as 'I am,'

and the past birth is completely forgotten.

The spirit is universal

and the mind is universal.

Only the ego creates a sense

of being individual.

It individualizes universal spirit

and the mind loses its own reality.

The more we identify ourselves

with worldly ego,

the more our problems

and confusion develop.

The more we identify with pure intellect,

the more our intellect discovers

the Self within.

The objects that are seen
cannot be separated from the seer.
The seer is aware of the objects seen,
but not aware of itself.

lly to all. Esto

t for everyone

houghts and ac

for   gr

Mind

y things you

tached to the

eace within

This peace is

ep a calm m

Mind is like a mirror

in which divine light reflects.

If the mirror is dirty,

it will not reflect the light.

When the idea of individuality

dawns in the mind,

the mind loses its identity

with the real Self,

and creates its own bondage.

When it tires of this bondage,

the mind seeks for the real Self,

which is always present and was never lost.

The three faculties of the mind,
understanding, passion, and ignorance,
are illumined by the energy of the Self.
The Self is inactive, independent,
and self-luminous.

Mind functions by suppression
and expression of thoughts.
Neither can it suppress all thoughts,
nor can it express all thoughts.
Therefore, in all identifications,
the mind uses both.

The world is constituted

by the five subtle elements:

sound, touch, form, taste, and odor.

The subtle elements

are the objects of the senses,

which are the ears, skin, eyes, tongue,

and nose, respectively.

The senses are simply extensions of the mind.

So the world is only an extension of the mind.

Mind absorbed in materialism
cannot enjoy spiritualism.
Dispassion is a must.

Mind dwelling in anger
is like a smoldering fire of chaff.
It burns internally and slowly
and makes life miserable.

There is no Satan, hell, or evil

somewhere out there.

It's only our own mind

that becomes satanic

and instigates evil actions,

creating a hellish life.

If evil doers are forgiven,

but their actions are not forgotten,

then some day the mind

will take revenge.

Those with deluded mind

see only objects with

separate names and forms,

but the wise see the one uniting factor

in all diversities.

For example different shapes,

sizes, and names of clay pots are seen,

but the one uniting factor in all pots,

the clay, remains hidden.

A dark place is frightening,

but when lit, there is no fear.

Darkness within is also frightening,

but when purity of mind shines forth,

the fear is gone.

Negative memories of past actions
appear in the present as suffering.
But if the mind is detached from the past,
suffering in the present ends.

We own nothing

until the sense of ownership

is developed in the mind.

We say, "This is my house,"

when we buy it.

The house has not changed,

only our sense of ownership

has developed.

Don't let the mind

be an enemy of the body.

Negative thoughts and self-hatred

only punish the body.

The forms of objects

that are identified by the mind and senses

create our world.

When that identification is stopped,

the world in the mind falls apart.

Fixity of mind on God comes

when all worldly thoughts fall dead.

Just as a rocky hill

is not shaken by a strong breeze,

a steady mind is not shaken

by a gust of desires.

Carrying a heavy backpack
with a positive frame of mind
doesn't reduce its weight,
but the person carries it happily.
Carrying a backpack
with a negative frame of mind,
makes it feel heavier all the time.
Carrying the load of life in the world
with complete acceptance
makes it easier to live.

Karma and
Samskara

Latent impressions, *samskaras,*
are deep imprints in the mind
caused by our actions,
thoughts, and feelings.
They are passed on birth to birth
and act as cause and effect.

Latent impressions

are like seeds that germinate

in favorable soil and climate.

We carry all of our latent impressions

all the time, but according to situations and

conditions, only the *samskaras* conducive to

action become operative.

Without favorable soil, latent impressions

remain dormant.

We inherit mental conditioning
from the past life, from the teachings
of our parents, from society, and
from our religious beliefs.
In this way we live as our elders lived.
Only if one is cabable of deconditioning
the mind from all old beliefs, dogmas,
and the latencies of the past,
can one find eternal truth.

Work itself is neither good nor bad,

but the motive that instigates us to act

determines the merits

or demerits of every action.

Providence neither favors nor disfavors.

It is our own karmas

that bring success or failure,

pleasure or pain.

No one is cut off

from divine grace at any time.

lly to all. Esto

t for everyone,

houghts and a

for   gr

y things   you

ttached to the

eace within.

Their peace is

eep a calm m

Death

A fruit has three layers:

outer skin, pulp or juice, and the seed.

The human body also has three layers:

the gross body, the energy body,

and the seed body.

The gross body dies, but the energy and

the seed bodies don't die.

They simply reincarnate, just as

the seed of a fruit makes a new tree.

Birth and death are as real

as sunrise and sunset.

Birth is celebrated by cheers

of happiness, but death

is faced by fear and mourning.

Birth is seen as a moment of happiness and

death appears as a great tragedy.

But both are two ends

of the same rope.

Anyone who has taken birth

will die for sure.

It is a well-known fact.

But out of fear

no one likes to think

about one's own death.

We are conscious

that someday we will die.

If we veil that consciousness of death,

then we die in fear.

Destruction and construction

make a cycle of creation.

Destruction of one

leads to construction

of the other.

Birth, growth, decay, and death

are the laws of nature.

Those who truthfully accept

the laws of nature

live in the present and

die in the present.

Self-Development

If you wish for spiritual development,

then start now and never stop.

Don't wait for an auspicious day to come.

Lofty spiritual ideas

may seem to be unattainable.

But by firm determination,

devotion, and enthusiastic effort

one can achieve the goal.

If you have to hike to a mountain top,

then you walk through the hills and dales,

woods and rivers, snowy cliffs and ravines.

You face all the odds and make it to the top.

The spiritual path is not a highway.

Neither hanker after the objects

that give experience of pleasure,

nor shun those objects that cause pain.

Allow them to be as a matter of course,

then one can achieve equanimity.

If you face life truthfully,

whether the situation is joyful

or full of misery, and

if you take responsibility for your actions,

be they negative or positive,

there will be reality in life

and it will save you

from psychological traumas.

One who is wearing clean white pants

avoids sitting on a dirty place.

In the same way one who is pure

in thoughts and actions avoids

negative thoughts and selfish actions.

The tightrope walker moves, swings,

and jumps on the rope,

but never misses her step.

A wise person in the world

acts in many ways,

but never steps on a wrong path.

Obstacles

in our spiritual development

originate from within,

but we project onto them

an outer cause.

Lust, anger, and greed

are three gateways to hell.

Lust gives rise to attachment,

anger gives rise to aversion,

and greed gives rise to discontentment.

Keep these three doors shut

for your self-development.

Attachment

brings manifold miseries

by creating anger,

hate, pride, and jealousy,

all of which

block one's self-development.

Self-betrayal starts when
we become selfish and irresponsible,
avoiding efforts for our self-development.

Evils are those thoughts and actions
that block one's self-development.

The evils in life are removed
by living a disciplined life
and by performing selfless service.

We are free to shape our own destiny,

but we become our own enemy

by indulging in lust, addictions,

and selfishness.

As we are inside, so we are outside.

Our inner development

is reflected in our actions,

behavior, speech, and

social adjustment.

It is not a sin if you have to lie or

tell an untrue story for the good of others,

because your motive is selfless and pure.

We live in a self-created, illusory world.
Study of scripture and
reflection expose it
and reveal the supreme reality
of the Self within.

If we are not aware of ourselves,

we cannot progress.

Don't back away if you don't succeed.

Failure strengthens

the foundation of your effort.

Stand up and try again.

Success is achieved by the force of will.

The world is kaleidoscopic

and impermanent.

One who has shunned attachment

to the impermanent

finds the way to God.

Purity in thought,

purity in speech,

and purity in action

bring divine presence in the heart.

Cultivate a sympathetic heart,

humility in dealings,

and selflessness in action.

If these are practiced

with earnestness and sincerity,

then you will win the race of life.

Karma yoga

Actions motivated by spiritual ideals
are the highest activities in life.

Karma Yoga, selfless service,
prepares us to live a divine life
because all of our self-interests
in the world are renounced.

The spirit of selfless service never stops.
You become an instrument of God
and work goes on.

If selfish action is

the cause of all miseries,

then selfless service

is the way to remove

those miseries

and bring peace.

By living life in the world
with a spirit of selfless service,
the mind develops devotion to God.
Only then, real surrender takes place
and "not my will, but thy will be done"
becomes a reality.

To serve others
with no selfish motive is sacrifice.
To give what others need
with no strings attached is charity.
To live a disciplined life is austerity.
Sacrifice, charity, and austerity together
in action is called Karma Yoga.

When the spirit

of selfless service is understood,

one engages oneself in serving humanity,

irrespective of class, color, or country.

Selfless service is a gift of God.

Those who have

that gift bestowed on them

are freed from all pain and misery.

lly to all. Esto

t for everyone

hou   ac

fu   gr

y   ou

ttached to the

eace within

Their peace is

eep a calm o

Love and Compassion

Unconditional love is universal love.

Universal love is the nature of God.

One who is established

in unconditional love

has found God.

Compassion is a heart filled
with feelings of sympathy
for the sufferer.

Compassion

becomes the nature of a person

who feels the pain of others

in his or her own heart.

Soft words of sympathy

at the right moment can restore

a depressed person's mind to vigor.

Love is a light

that emanates from the heart

and removes all differences,

separation, and self-interest.

Love is free from all conditions.

It shines equally for everyone,

like the light of the sun.

But one who sits in a dark corner

can't experience it.

Love is a universal religion.

Pure love has no lust.

Lust is the craving of the senses,

and pure love is

the expression of the soul.

Love and hate are two opposites.

If one is capable of removing hate within,

then love will emanate without.

Love for the small self

veils the divine within.

Love for the divine Self

reveals the divinity in everything.

In the presence of a sage

who is established in universal love,

a spiritually dead person comes alive and

a spiritually blind person starts seeing.

We love where the love is returned;

where the love is not responded to,

indifference is a natural result.

But one who loves

without expecting love in return

is loving God in all beings.

Simplicity in nature,

greatness in character,

compassion in action,

and love for all

are gifts from God.

Rare are the ones

who are ready to receive them.

lly to all. Esto

t for everyone

houghts and ac

for **Guru** e gr

y things you

ttached to the

eace within

This peace is

eep a calm m

Guru is one who is higher in knowledge
and capable of transmitting that knowledge
by words, action, or just by being.
But the real guru is the pure consciousness
that dwells in the heart of everyone.

Guru can point to the right path,

but can't tread it for others.

The seeker has to go through

a painful struggle to achieve the goal.

It's only vanity when a guru
claims to take someone's karmas.
No one can eat for any one else.

A prejudiced listener
either doesn't pay attention
to the teachings of a teacher,
or understands the contrary
of what was said.
Only one who is pure in mind
really listens.

Experience is a great teacher.

A child who once burned his finger

in a candle flame

doesn't try to touch it again;

from a safe distance,

he blows air to put out the flame.

The archer, whose concentration

gets fixed on the target,

hits the target.

One who only looks

at the bow and arrow fails.

Similarly, one who gets fixed

on the teachings of the guru

achieves the aim,

but not the one

who simply follows the physical guru.

The spiritual guru in a physical form
is a reminder of your spiritual path.

The inner guru teaches
with the voice of silence.
Impure mind hears it not.
Some listen, but trust it not.

163

When the outer guru's teachings
and the inner guru's silent whisper
appear the same,
then the seeker's faith
gets fixed without any doubts.

lly to all. Esto
t for everyone.
houghts and a
few Devotion gr
y things you
ttached to the
eace within
Their peace is
eep a calm o

Devotion to God means
intense love for God.
There is supreme longing for God.
It is practiced by contemplation
of divine powers, wisdom, and goodness,
by keeping the divine presence within,
by continuous remembrance,
by reading about God's glories,
by chanting God's praise,
by listening to stories of God,
and by performing all acts
as service to God.
In this way, the human soul
is pulled closer to the divine.

God is beyond name and form,

an all-pervasive energy.

But our worship of God

in a form, with faith and devotion,

makes that form divine.

Giving a name and form to God

has a purpose.

God is worshipped

by means of name and form,

and this worship leads to

the ultimate realization

of the supreme truth.

The human incarnation

is the highest incarnation,

yet it is limited in power.

Faith in God, who is omnipotent,

is the only support.

Life in the world

is like walking on quicksand;

the more you try to get out,

the deeper you sink.

Only by the grace of God

can one avoid the quicksand.

A blooming flower, not a faded one,

is offered to God as a mark of devotion.

Offer yourself to God

when you are blooming in life.

A mind filled with negative thoughts
is a diseased mind.
It is cured by engaging the mind
in devotion to God.

The mind takes the form
of the object perceived.
If the mind is engaged
in the worship of God
with faith and devotion,
then it will take the form
of the God worshipped.

One whose mind is free

from anger, greed, and pride,

and who is leading a life

of absolute purity

is treading the path of devotion,

whether the person is a theist

or an atheist.

A wise person's devotion to God

is for achieving eternal peace.

An ignorant person's devotion to God

is for achieving worldly pleasures.

At the time of failure,

when depression sets in,

don't desert your devotion

to your spiritual aim.

Then you will succeed.

Only the visionary potter
can see different varieties of pots
and toys in a clay lump.
Similarly, a visionary devotee alone
sees various divine forms
in phenomenal nature.

A paper kite high up in the sky,

tied with a string,

is supported by the air from all sides.

Similarly, one who has achieved

Self-knowledge

is tied by the string of devotion to God,

even while moving around.

Without a perpetual sense
of dedication to God,
neither philosophies,
nor study of scriptures,
nor meditation
will enlighten your heart
and bring eternal peace.

Hold your faith and devotion steadfastly,

keep your mind steady in self-discipline,

build your endurance

by observing austerities,

then you can't fall from the path.

Repetition of a divine name

or a sacred syllable

brings the mind into the present

where there is no past or future,

only divine presence.

One who is devoted

to one's spiritual ideals,

develops indifference

to all pairs of opposites,

like success or failure,

praise or ignominy,

good fortune or misfortune.

Spiritual aim is like a compass

that points toward God.

No matter how much

the compass is turned around,

its direction never changes.

The omnipresent divine Lord

cannot hide from us.

We are the ones

who hide behind the veil

of our egocentric desires.

Controlling thought waves
in order to attain *samadhi*
is the hardest of all austerities.
Living in devotional thoughts
easily connects one with God.

Devotion is a state of mind

in which love for the beloved

flows unceasingly.

Devotion is not time-bound.

It is an unconditional love.

By the grace of God,

when higher intuition unfolds within,

it brings a knowledge that is beyond

the realm of this world reality;

it is unexplainable

and can only be experienced.

Our prayers will be heard
and favorable fruit will be bestowed
only when we pray with pure mind
and devoted heart.

God is love, light, and peace.

Those who love God wholeheartedly

receive the gift of love from God.

Worship the Lord with devotion.

Go deeper and deeper into it.

Experience more and more

the truth behind devotion.

Let that state take over your psyche

and you will merge

in the bliss of the divine.

lly to all. Esto

t for everyone

houghts and ar

surrender qu

y things you

tached to the

eace within

This peace is

eep a calm or

Taking refuge in God

means to offer all of your actions,

thoughts, feelings, and emotions to God.

You do not remain a doer.

You are free and liberated from

your own self-created bondage.

We cannot have peace,

happiness, and contentment

until we offer our hearts

to the Divine

and become one with it.

At the time of despondency,

pain, gloominess, or hopelessness,

where can you turn?

Let your mind be fixed on God

with complete surrender.

We suffer in the present
by simply dwelling
in our painful memories.
If we take refuge in God,
we are no longer our past
and no longer the sufferer.

We should welcome

the pain that motivates us

to search for God,

just as we would take poison

to cure a sickness.

In any life threatening situation,

in which one has no defense

and no remedy,

the desperate mind turns to prayer.

That prayer is from the heart and it is

listened to by God.

Even if one sits in a cave

or lives in the woods,

one is not taking refuge in God

as long as the ego of being a performer

is alive in the heart.

Surrender to God

and God will take care of you.

You can either cling to God

as a baby monkey clings to its mother,

or let God carry you along

as a cat carries her helpless kitten.

With each sunrise and sunset
our life is reduced by a day.
For one who has taken refuge in God,
nothing is lost.
The devotee is always with God
whether alive or dead.

God's love showers down on humanity.

Those who surrender to God with devotion

give that love back to God.

lly to all. Esto
t for everyone
houghts and a
for   gr
y things you
ttached to the
eace within
This peace is
ef a calm or

yoga

Yoga is not a physical exercise.
It is finding yourself within yourself
by removing worldly thoughts
from the mind.

When one is merged

in worldly enjoyments,

one is enslaved by

the blind force of attachment.

Regular practice of yoga

is the rescuer.

205

When the objective mind
is disciplined and works in unity
with the subjective mind,
it is called yoga.
This yoga is achieved by the
removal of egocentric desires.

Clear perception of the truth, egolessness,

and eternal satisfaction

is a state of *samadhi*,

whether the spiritual aspirant works

in the world or sits in a cave.

When body, breath, and mind,

work together in harmony

to achieve a spiritual goal,

that is yoga.

As long as concentration

is consciously flowing,

it is meditation.

When that conscious effort subsides

and the mind merges in the Self,

it is *samadhi.*

meditation

When God is loved
and continuously remembered,
that is meditation.

Practicing meditation
on a regular basis
is like wiping the dust
from a mirror every day.
In a clean mirror
you can see yourself clearly.
Similarly, in the clean mind
the Self is seen.

Meditation

is not getting lost

in imagination;

it is merging into

the thought of the divine.

Scattered mind

comes together by meditation.

One-pointed mind

unties the knot of ignorance,

and wisdom dawns.

A candle flame flickers
where there is wind;
similarly, the mind gets restless
when breath is abnormal.

One who has lost touch

with the center

of his or her being becomes

restless, confused, and depressed.

One gets back in touch with that center

by contemplation.

A magician attracts the mind
of the audience by magic tricks;
the audience gets absorbed in the show,
and the world is forgotten.
Similarly, when the mind is absorbed in God,
the world disappears.

Pilgrimage, charity,

living in seclusion are good for

one's self-development;

but if you are seeking for divine truth,

or God, then contemplate the Self.

The infinite
divine manifestation
of innumerable objects
is recognized by one-pointed
contemplation.

Think of the absolute, infinite,

eternal God as the goal of life.

Contemplate on the light of the divine

with faith and surrender.

Let your mind be fixed on that light.

Worldly desires, attachments,

and greed may rise in your thoughts.

Ignore them.

Be persistent in withdrawing
your mind from the world,
from anger, fear, hate,
jealousy, attachment, and pride.
Remove malice from your heart.
Be friendly to all.
Establish love in your heart for everyone.
Be selfless in your thoughts and actions.

Be humble and seek for divine grace.

Don't get agitated by things you don't like.

Don't get attached to things you like.

Sit in peace within and peace without.

This peace is the divine light.

Keep a calm mind and

contemplate the divine light.

Renunciation
and Dispassion

One whose aim

is to attain eternal peace,

who is not a threat

to society or individuals,

and who is consciously engaged in

his or her own self-development

is a renunciate,

even though living in society.

A thorn in the foot

is pulled out by a needle,

not by a cotton wick.

Deep-rooted ignorance is removed

by the sword of dispassion,

not by the romance of attachment.

Only renunciation of
all notions of 'I' and 'mine,'
is true renunciation.

Giving up the sense

of self-importance, attachment,

and self-interest

in one's thoughts is renunciation.

Renunciation in action alone

and not in thoughts is falsehood.

lly to all. Esto

t for everyone

houghts and a

for   the gr

y things you

ttached to the

eace within

This peace is

eep a calm an

self

The essential nature of fire

is heat and light;

without heat and light, fire doesn't exist.

The essential nature

of human beings is the divine Self;

without the divine Self

humanity would not exist.

Yet we don't know our essential nature

because this Self is obscured

by worldly experiences.

The consciousness
that illumines the mind,
the intellect, and the senses
is that divine energy
which is called the Self.

The nature of the Self,

the pure conscious principle,

is self-luminous.

It is that light which illumines

the mind and intellect,

as well as the knower and the known.

The Self is the conscious principle

present in all changes

that take place in life.

But the Self remains unchanged,

inactive, pure, and self-luminous.

The self-luminous,

pure conscious principle,

in the presence of which

everything comes to light,

is the Self.

The same Self,

when rooted in the mind,

becomes the individual self.

The Self is the essence of life force,

without which nothing exists.

In the mind, it takes the form

of consciousness;

in the body, it takes the form

of energy.

Spirit and matter create the body.

Spirit is like a color,

which dyes matter by its pervasive nature.

Matter is finite and always changing.

As it pervades matter, spirit

goes through all material changes

and thereby loses its independence.

The body exists

in triple aspects:

gross, subtle, and causal.

God also exists in a being

in triple aspects:

the ego-self, the embodied Self,

and the supreme conscious principle

or pure Self.

Within the three aspects of the body
are five sheaths: the physical sheath,
the vital or energy sheath,
the mental sheath, the intellect sheath,
and the bliss sheath.
These sheaths cognize the world.
This five-fold body is illumined
by the divine principle without which
the body has no cognizing ability.

The notion of 'I am' takes birth
with the body and dies with the body.
But when one loses the mortal ego of
'I am this mind-body complex,'
one becomes immortal
as 'I am the Self' is revealed.

Everything is revealed
by the light of the Self.
The Self is revealed by its own light,
not by the light of the mind and intellect.

Just as a thick cloud covers the sun,

blocking its light and heat,

the mind-body complex

hides the glory of the Self.

A boat and its navigator are separate,

yet they work together;

without one, the other has no function.

Similarly, the body and the soul

are different and yet they work together;

without one the other doesn't function.

The Self is the sovereign;

nature is its kingdom;

mind and intellect are ministers;

and ego is the governor,

which rules for its own self-interest.

SELF

The Self is neither a performer of action
nor the enjoyer of the fruit of action.
It is neither born nor ever dies.
When it reflects on the mind and intellect,
it appears to be a performer and enjoyer,
taking birth and dying.

When a red hot iron is hammered,

it takes different shapes,

but the red hot flame remains the same.

Similarly when the ego-self

in one's life goes through changes,

like pleasure, pain, and fear,

the pure Self remains unchanged.

I am known by my name
and form, actions, and emotions.
But the real 'I' is unknown.
'I' is known when the concept of
'I am this mind-body complex'
is removed.

By bravery and intelligence,

a soldier in the battlefield

gets promoted higher and higher

and eventually becomes a general.

Yet it is the same person

who was a soldier and became a general.

Similarly, when the ego wins

the battle of desires and attachments,

it becomes the Self.

A dreamer can't be separated
from the dream until waking.
Similarly, 'I' can't be separated
from 'I am-ness' until
achieving Self-knowledge.

When the mind
honestly accepts that 'I'
do not belong to objects,
thoughts, or feelings,
nor do they belong to me,
the 'I' becomes isolated.
That 'I' is the Self.

The darkness

of the mind

is dispelled

by the light of the soul,

which is knowledge of the Self.

The ego of individuality

is not divine nature.

The ego of universality

is divine nature.

Meditate on universal Self.

It is pure and eternal.

Thick green moss
covers the surface of a pond.
A heavy gust of wind
pushes the moss away to the banks
and clean water is seen.
The ego with its multitude of forms
covers the Self.
Supreme dispassion blows away the ego
and the Self is seen in its pristine glory.

lly to all. Esto

t for everyone

houghts and ac

for silence gr

y change you

tached to the

eace within

This peace is

ep a calm or

Silence is the eternal nature.

Sound appears with creation,

and when creation dissolves,

it disappears.

It is just like darkness,

in which light appears with sunrise

and disappears with sunset.

Beyond time, space, and causation
is silence.
That silence is Brahman, the Absolute.
In that silence, sound starts
by the movement of energies,
and it creates forms.
That primordial sound, which is Om,
is the mother of creation.

Sound originates from silence,

speech originates from sound.

When speech is controlled,

it brings inner silence.

The great Spirit is identified within

by silencing the mind,

not merely by silencing speech.

The soul speaks with a voice of silence.

Physical ears hear it not.

Only the pure mind

understands that voice.

lly to all. Esto

t for everyone

houghts and a

tow   e gr

Peace

y things   you

tached to the

ace within

This peace is

ep a calm m

The purpose of human incarnation

is to achieve eternal peace.

Keep the purpose of life in mind.

Work hard to achieve your goal.

Nonviolence in the mind

and unconditional love in the heart

bring eternal peace.

Nonviolence

is the supreme path

to peace,

within and without.

Dwelling in past memories
is the cause of pain in the present.
Living in the present,
unrelated to the past and future,
is living in peace.

When the mind is free

from all past memories

and imaginary cognitions

about the future,

it is in the present

where there is perfect peace.

One who has no enemy in the world,

who is devoid of hope and fear,

who is without pride and violent thoughts,

attains eternal peace.

Such a person is joyful everywhere

in all situations.

Peace in the mind,

love and compassion in the heart

bring the scattered world

into one reality.

lly to all. Esto
t for everyone
houghts and a
for   e gr

Truth

y things you
ttached to the
eace within
This peace is
ep a calm n

Ordinary mind
perceives surface truths,
but enlightened mind
sees the inner Truth
that doesn't change.

The finite,

or the world of objects,

is ever changing.

The infinite, or pure consciousness,

knows no change.

Without the present
there can't be past or future.
Knowing the present,
which is eternal,
is knowing the Truth.

Movement in space

is measured by time.

If movement stops,

time also stops.

The human mind

is always looking for something satisfying.

Even those who have enormous wealth,

fame, and power crave it.

It remains unknown

until one dives deep within

and finds the divine spark

that brings contentment.

In every step of life

we are cheating ourselves

because of our self-interest,

motives, desires, and attachments.

Remove all those veils,

which are created by our mind,

and peek outside.

Then you will know Truth,

which is beyond the mind's illusion.

Knowledge and ignorance

are like grain and chaff.

In winnowing, the grain falls in the basket

and the chaff flies away.

True knowledge is the grain,

which is useful;

ignorance is the chaff,

which is useless.

Eyes perceive the outer realities;

mind perceives the inner realities.

As long as the mind

is busy with sense perceptions,

it will never find the inner Truth.

Don't try to convert anyone to your beliefs.

Let people choose their own path.

If your heart is pure and mind is clear,

then people will follow your footsteps.

For one who is established in Truth,

life in the world

becomes an act that only looks real,

like a drama on the stage.

When one achieves

knowledge of the Truth,

the facts of the past

become fictions in the present.

The lamp of wisdom
lit inside is not showing
Truth to you alone;
it is also shared by others
who are in your proximity.

The cosmic energy,

which is continuously creating

and annihilating the macrocosm,

as well as the microcosm,

is divine energy known as God.

Divine God

is beyond space and time

and yet pervades space and time.

So God is absent in everything

and yet present in everything.

lly to all. Esto

t for everyone

houghts and a

liberation.

y things you

ttached to the

eace within

This peace is

eep a calm a

Stable aim, faith, devotion,

and one-pointed contemplation on God

is the path of yoga through which

one achieves liberation.

Bondage and liberation
are two concepts.
When the mind is possessed
by the idea 'I am this body,'
that is bondage.
When that idea is changed to
'I am the Self,'
that is liberation.

Liberation is prevented
by our own false identification
with the mind-body complex.
As soon as this illusory identification
is removed, we merge into the Absolute.

'I am this mind-body complex'
is self-conditioning.
The conditioned mind
creates bondage of the soul;
deconditioning of the mind
is its liberation.
The minds of those who
are born with faith and devotion
are also conditioned;
but it is a spiritual conditioning
and it eliminates worldly conditioning.

As long as the notion

of individuality exists

in thoughts, actions, and feelings,

one cannot be said to be liberated.

The notion of individuality

itself is bondage.

I-consciousness is in *buddhi* (the mind)

and creates the idea of individuality.

If that I-consciousness is removed,

then the mind identifies with

undifferentiated consciousness, the Self,

and merges in it.

That is liberation of the embodied soul.

God, world, and the Self
are identified as separate realities
by the ego working through the mind.
If the ego is absent in the mind, then
there remains pure consciousness alone,
a state of nonduality.

Scientific knowledge

proves the cause and effect

of worldly matters

and dispels ignorance of the mind.

Science of the soul goes beyond the mind

and dispels the ignorance

that veils the soul.

Then ultimate Truth is realized.

When charcoal powder

is poured into molten bronze,

it burns up the dross as well as itself.

Similarly, supreme dispassion

burns all impurities of the mind

and then burns itself.

There remains nothing except God.

Joy and sorrow,

hope and despair,

life and death,

are experienced in a dream.

Upon waking one simply says,

"It was not real, it was a dream."

Similarly, upon waking

from the state of ignorance,

one identifies past experiences

as a dream.

All is imperfect in human incarnation
except that bright essence of the soul,
which is eternal.
When that eternal spirit is identified,
human incarnation is freed
from its imperfection,
birth and death.

The descent of God

into a human form

is a God-incarnated soul.

Realization of that God within

is the liberation of the human soul.

A spark of fire

quickly burns down a heap of dry grass.

A spark of divine knowledge

burns a heap of desires and expectations in

a moment.

Physical death

is the cause of rebirth,

but death of the ego

is the cause of liberation from

the cycle of birth and death.

Several roads lead to the same town.

Similarly, different spiritual paths

lead to liberation.

Only the paths are different,

but not the liberation.

One who is curious

to know "Who am I"?

"Why am I here"?

seriously looks within,

deeply ponders, and sets out on the

pilgrimage of liberation.

The purpose

of the embodied human soul

is to go back to

the over-soul from where

it originally came.

The journey is long

but not time-bound.

Faith in God,

love in the heart,

compassion in the mind,

and effort with enthusiasm

open the door of liberation.

To enter into the kingdom of God
there are four gates:
Persistent practice of yoga with faith,
Selfless service,
Cultivation of virtuous qualities,
Surrender to God.

A beam of light

coming through a tiny hole

in the roof

makes light in the room.

Similarly,

a beam of consciousness

coming through pure intellect

enlightens the whole psyche.

God is infinite and unknown.

The knower

simply merges in the unknown.

When the mind attains eternal peace,

that is God.

When the mind attains supreme Truth,

that is God.

When the mind attains complete silence,

that is God.

Any one of these mental states

leads to liberation.

One who identifies the Self within
is freed from worldly allurements,
praise, and pride.

Only those with the eye of wisdom

can see the other bank of the river of life.

It is away from the world

and exists in God alone.

One who has achieved eternal peace
encounters no restlessness, boredom,
or lustful desires,
because the mind is merged in
the blissful nature of the soul.

One who is endowed
with Self-knowledge
never remains inactive,
idle, or inert.
Such a person remains busy
in selfless service.

One is *jivan mukta* (liberated while alive)

who has shunned

all attachments to the world

and its evolutes, experiences,

emotions, and sentiments.

Just as the sun

demands nothing in return

for offering its light and heat,

the enlightened being

demands nothing

for offering spiritual knowledge.

Nonviolence

is the supreme duty of a human being.

One who is established in nonviolence

in thoughts, actions, and speech

is standing on the threshold

of liberation.

The mind, body, and senses
of a liberated being
function perfectly without the sense
that 'I am this mind-body complex.'

When hankering for sense pleasure ceases,

when the heart grieves for

the miseries of others

and rejoices in the happiness of others,

when the mind is free from vanity and passion

and cherishes guileless devotion to God,

such a soul is called a saint.

Enlightened and ignorant people
look the same and act the same;
but the enlightened person
remains unattached to actions,
whereas the ignorant person
becomes attached.

The path of devotion
is a path of love, worship, and surrender.
It is a path of duality.
But when one's mind, intellect, and ego
are completely merged in God,
then what is left except God?
A nondual state.

Nonduality is a state of mind;
it is not expressed in action.

Self-knowledge is eternal peace
in which the search is over.
This peace is an eternal action
in which there is no self-interest.
It is a divine activity that never stops.

By abandoning all notions,
conditionings, and conceptions,
there remains nothing
except the divine light
emanating from the heart.

Ashtanga Yoga Primer

Cat & Sparrow

A Child's Garden of Yoga

Essays 1 — Binding Thoughts & Liberation

Essays 2 — Mind is Our World

Essays 3 — Selfless Service: the Spirit of Karma Yoga

Fire Without Fuel

Hairakhan Baba — Known, Unknown

The Magic Gem — A Story-Coloring Book

Mystic Monkey

Silence Speaks: from the Chalkboard of Baba Hari Dass

Sweeper to Saint—Stories of Holy India

The Yellow Book (out of print)

Vinaya Chalisa

Anjali — Melodies of Ancient India

Guru Purnima Songs

Horizons — Improvisations for Harp and Flute

Inner Light — Improvisations on East Indian Melodies

Jai Govinda!

Jai Ma Kirtan — Songs to the Divine Mother

Jai Shiva! Kirtan for Shivaratri

Jaya Shambho

Murali Krishna

Songs of the Ramayana

Sri Ram Kirtan — Volumes I & II

Tender Mercies — Hanuman Fellowship Women's Choir

For free catalog write:
Sri Rama Publishing
P.O. Box 2550
Santa Cruz, CA 95063

The profits from the sale of Babaji's books

and the musical recordings produced by

Sri Rama Publishing, are used to directly

support Shri Ram Orphanage in India.

Founded by Baba Hari Dass, Shri Ram provides

a loving home for needy and orphaned children.

Shri Ram's school and free health clinic serve

our children as well as families of nearby villages.

For further information please contact Sri Rama

Foundation, PO Box 2550, Santa Cruz, CA, 95063